Borrowed

Space

A novel in verse by Kay Caswell

To the kids who thought themselves painfully average because they never heard their stories told.

And to the reader, don't worry about reading this in order. We all handle life in different paces and patterns.

"That is the exploration that awaits you! Not mapping stars or studying nebula, but charting the unknown possibilities of existence."

- Leonard Nimoy.

Welcome to Dodham University!

It is always my greatest honor to welcome new students to our campus! Here in the quiet town of Dodham Illinois, forty-five minutes north of Chicago, our university of around 6,500 students sits not far from two great worlds: quiet town life and one of the largest urban locations in the entire United States. We at Dodham pride ourselves on being an incredibly diverse and accepting home for students of all backgrounds. All of our majors are run by professors and administrators who hope to best prepare you for work in the professional world, whether it be in the arts, the corporate world, or an intersection of the two.

Our staff hopes that all of you are excited for this semester, beginning on September 3rd. Here is a final reminder to all incoming students that move-in day is August 27th, so please check the attached information pertaining to dorm locations. Also, remember to turn in all of your physical examination forms by August 1st and register for all of your classes by August 15th. We can not wait to see all of you at the end of this summer!

                                            Best Regards,
                                    Carol Richardson, Dean of Students

Fall Semester

September 3rd - December 18th

Garret Marshall

Bruiser

It takes fewer than ten minutes
to shave a full head of curls,
and the same amount of time
to make sure my chest is properly bound.
Tight like a nail bolt,
keeping me grounded, but still
letting me breathe.
It takes two minutes to put on
my cargo shorts, lace up my shoes,
button my shirt.
My hips jolt out like waves onto a
shore. I try not to mind.
I'm leaving with mom and dad
out of sight. They can't see me off-
they're working and all-
but mom's apple butter still burns
a hole in my carry-on and my head
spins on and off the freeway as I
wrap it around the word
"campus" but at least my student
ID reads,
"Dodham University Student
Garret Marshall
Gender: Male"

He's a Guy

I pull the towel up to cover my chest,
hide my eyes from the rubber bodies
of flattened muscle-bound glory.
They can't see me that way.
They can't see the water dripping down
my breasts, covered in stretch marks from
puberty like the fat around my hips but
every time they see me in here they
remind each other "he's a guy" because
the boys' bathrooms are for us guys
and no matter how many skinny dudes
call me a dyke I'm still a boy who needs
to hide his body beneath baggy clothes
and mildewy towels or the only
baggy thing to cover me will be
zippered shut and driven to the Morgue.

Crummy Work Ethic

I can't remember the last time
I fell asleep in double digit time, with
the "PM" trailing the 4 numbers in
its happily reasonable way because
"3:32 AM" just seems far more familiar
at this point, with cookie crumbs on my face
and the smell of coffee staining my dreams
like how the computer keys print on my cheeks
because I don't know how to fall asleep anywhere else.
The dorm advisors put me here alone
anyway for my safety so the sleep schedule of a room mate
is of no concern, good for when the Big Paper
is due tomorrow and I've barely hit two
hundred words. Maybe two hundred
is a good time to take a break? Maybe
I can stop and look up some microwave
cookie recipes because if there's one
thing that college has taught me, it's that
anything can be done with a microwave.

Don't Insult Me, Mystery Meat

The Gingham Dining Hall is not known to many
as the pinnacle of culinary innovation, so when I look
down at a plate of "meatloaf" I'm not mad,
just disappointed like a father who found out his son cheated
on his math test. By that argument one could say that
food is my child, which would be preposterous
because food is a broad concept but it is one
my stomach takes ever-so-seriously.
When I look out at the frat boys walking to the King of all Burgers
I can't help but think "is this really how low we've stooped here,
mystery meatloaf? Is a fast food sandwich preferable to
your graces?" but by this point I realize that I'm internally
monologue-ing to a piece of blended cow intestines when I could be
grabbing a slip from the tear-away "Help Wanted" sign
before where the non-existent lunch line begins, adjacent to the
parfaits emitting foul smells.

Cash or Class?

My mental resume reads,
"No time available, busy student.
4 o'clock am and I have become
synonymous."
So how in God's Green Earth
am I supposed to handle a job?
"Local Lazy Boy makes Life Way Harder
for a Bit of Extra Cash, Wants
Chest Surgery so He Won't Need
to Bind Anymore."
The cafeteria could actually show its face
with me behind the stove,
but could I even stand or would I be
face-down on the burners as if they're
computer keyboards that I mistake
for pillows?
Will I trade more hours of sleep
just so I won't feel like my chest is going to
burst? Who knows what I can do?

Ricochet

They told me to be a dish washer.
They want me to be the asshole
who cleans off some shitty
mystery meat from some kid's
plate. I'm a first year student yes,
not like I'd get ahead of myself,
but I hold myself higher than two dollars
an hour and lunch scraps.
Especially when I live like this,
barely concealing breasts that hormone
replacement can't even hide; paying
for treatment in the first place,
living off convenience store noodles,
hiding at parties away from the boys
who think I'm artificial.

Kitchen Blues

There's a mouse looking up at me from
the sink. He's from the enclave behind
the cabinets where the mousey
democracy votes on whose turn it is
to run out and steal some food.

There's Jared, the guy with the cleanest apron
and voice like tennis shoes on a gym floor.
He reminds me that there's grease on the
plates, meat crumbles are dancing on
imposter-china.

There's Rowen, a pink haired pessimist
who sits in the corner on her phone when
there's forks likes lightning rods and
she should be the germ-icidal storm.

There's me, wannabe chef-boy
with a heart of crumb cake and apple jam,
the pathetic patience of a hot tamale,
the dread of pea soup.

Getting Out

After work, a couple of other culinary
majors called me about a party,
down by the lake where tree branches
dip down just enough to slap you in the face.
But, I needed to get out.
I couldn't stay cooped up in a dorm room,
face in a bowl of soup and eyes strained
over some paper.

Instead, I saw plenty of faces,
familiar from crowds in the courtyard
and cafeteria, but still alarmingly unknown.
Some were tattooed with drunken red cheeks,
some opened their mouths wide enough
in laughter that I could practically smell
the nacho breath.

One sat alone, under the branches but
low enough to not get slapped in the face.
She looked like a blowfish ready to burst
with the words she has to say,
but no one to say them to.

Borrowed Space

The walls of around me are not my own,
they will hold some other kid's posters
a year from now.
The fields outside, stone walkways, benches,
fountains: none of them are mine.
How could they be when I've only passed
them for three months and I'm not even
close to knowing all the people they carry.
I do not yet have a Magnum Opus,
and I'm biding my time here until the day it happens
be it some successful restaurant,
job as a celebrity chef,
or just a college degree.
Until that day comes, I'm just sitting
in borrowed space, waiting for its
revelation in vivid Technicolor.

Gene Harper

Genie Green Bean

Insects crawl their way through the glass bottle,
up my biceps, triceps, nesting in my head,
reminding me of Genie Green Bean, the
me with no knuckles who got too used to
feeling the mulch digging into her knee caps
and the acid in her eyes after crying under the sun
but punching bags and brass knuckles
saved the day. Now I'm stuck in this world
of old white walls, crisp new bed sheets,
a room mate who smells like coffee and
bad decisions: those boys who can't
keep their mouths shut in her bed during the night
bound to wake up with black eyes
because I can't hear my own thoughts and
I'm a strong deviant with a beating heart
instead of scrawny little girl with noodle arms
and boiled cheeks.

Yuck

All of my paintings look like slime
and all of my boots are covered in dirt.
My tank tops are coated with stains
even after they're washed and I smell
like the thrift store; sugar and piss.
So when I see the angel down the hall,
girl of white lace and parfum
I can't hope to draw her eyes closer,
I'm too Blood and Guts
and I built myself this way, years
of bruises and sharpened nails,
so where is she going to go if I try to
make conversation and how would I
hold her hand when lightning runs
through my veins?

Figures of Speech

Blue hair dye stains my forehead
because maintaining the bangs leaves
me looking bruised and asking girls
for their numbers leaves me feeling
bruised but I can live with it when
I've got her digits in my palm. She told
me her name was Reena, after the
lecture in the hall that smells like mildew.
I can't tell if I want a relationship
because tying me down doesn't work
with even the prettiest rope but
I've got the date in my mind, we're
grabbing lunch next Saturday and I
feel new like fresh skin covering
used-to-be wounds and black hair
roots growing out a against a bleached
scalp. I guess this time I won't jump
ship like they always say, because
the ship heading on its unknown course
is still safer than the possibilities of
a saltwater ocean.

Tell Her the Baggage

One day in order for her to love me
I have to tell her about what I carry,
broken bones and black eyes,
bruised knuckles waking up 2 am in
a back alley, an ex lover's raised eyebrows
February 22nd on a gravestone,
eyes swollen against the granite
countertop, mad drunk madder hangover
old bus fares and the smell of
standing water under city overpasses
down by the river where I found
the body and why I don't talk to my
parents anymore, too scared to get my
driver's license because that makes it
easier to leave, I need to leave and I know
that there's no way in hell I'll ever tell
her.

Negatonin

I weave myself apart with
the pieces breaking down
next to a room mate trying to sleep
but I'm not allowed to sleep when
I draw back on old friends dancing
around with me, under the bridge
but over the water, where we laughed
like Fortune 500-ers, pocketing
billions from some
Service You Can Rely On
but our services were kicking buckets
until one of us took it too far and
now The Body From The River.
It who was he lies next to me,
"don't go to sleep when you could be
saving me, Genie in a Bottle,
grant me my wish and don't live
like the other tear drops
painting penises on cement walls.
They're real dicks, you know that
Genie Green-Bean? You're not
a gold-certified psycho like the rest."

Falling in Love on Halloween

I miss the light from neighbors' foyers,
hugging me with warmth even though
I was ghoulish; a witch, a demon.
I was only there to grab some candy and
fly to the next house,
haunting for some sugar.

Reena gives me honey eyes and
hugs like cashmere. She sees where
the sores are- stings from wasps
picking at my shell.

I want to go trick-or-treating again some day,
somewhere where college students can dress
up like ghoulish witches and demons to
haunt for sugar and hugs from not just light
but youth and love and all the colors in between.
I can bring Reena and kids from every
lint-coated couch and spring-pimpled mattress.

We can all trade treats and compliment costumes
like the kids up past their bedtimes that very night.
We can pretend that growing up doesn't happen too fast.

Classy

What does sophisticated mean?
Not passed out drunk in the student lounge?
No greasy blue bangs?
No art with entrails gushing out?
I speak French, you know.
I learned how to ballroom dance and
got an A in English back in the day.
I can wear a dress, hold my wine.
Boys at parties expect me to be a
walking train wreck, I've gotten
the reputation. They may have seen me
puking in a dumpster, but sometimes
that's life when you're depressed and careless
but I'm not beneath class.
Take me out where the four-course meals are,
I'll wear a dress of satin,
smoke with a cigarette holder,
discuss literature over chardonnay and
avoid the kitsch because
it's not where respect comes from.

Staying In

I need to learn more about that:
staying in where the bed sheets
are soft and new art can be made.
Instead, I know too much about
getting drunk and tripping over tree roots
in parks where boys watch for inhibition
and girls smack the ground
when they start to drown in hard liquor.

Sucks for me; inside is where
February 22nd lives. It rears its ugly head
when I'm in those soft bed-sheets and
done with all that art. It reminds me
that yes, an emotionally abusive friend
died and I still live with that date.

I've tried telling it we're through,
I've moved on and I'm seeing someone new,
but it still wants to tango.

Shelter from the Cold

The sun is in Sagittarius,
let's take December by storm.
I am in love and I am thriving,
I chopped inches off of my hair and
learned new names.
A girl named Lila, a face remembered
in static from a party,
sprouts anew in my life. She gave
me a small cactus and called me resilient.
She sits now with me and Reena,
down in the Gingham Dining hall
where sunlight drowns her when she
faces the window. She teaches me
of nature's deities, the ones who
help with fresh starts. I
will push on forward, smiling
at January's novelty,
and ignoring February as though
it's a passing phase. Thank the gods
that it's the shortest month of the year.

Reena Bateman

Petticoats don't travel Well

I place my luggage on my bed,
unzip and pull out dress by dress,
skirt by blouse by pair of pink heels,
lace among lace and pattern among pattern,
wrinkled frilly things to hang in the
stuffy grayscale closet like books
waiting to be read but closed upon a shelf.
A five-hour flight, New Jersey to Illinois,
and a bus ride along bumpy pebble roads
ruffled the tulle.
Pretty things like me don't travel well,
we get lost in the wrinkles like the
expensive frills and petticoats losing their
poof. Luckily enough, any outfit will look
refined and presentable
with a bit of dry cleaning and enough
patience.

Do Creepy Girls like to Dress up?

Her earbuds are too embedded in her head
for her to look over and see me
but I always flash a smile, wiggle my fingers,
I'd like to say hello
                      how are you?
                                    You're
very pretty but not halloween store spooky,
You're back alley, navy tone bruised bricks
and broken bottles housing rats and ripped
condoms spooky and I don't know if putting
a bow on you and calling you cute would
work. Not when I'm still using night lights
and worrying about how to say hi
                                    I'm Reena
I live in the dorm
                down the hall
                              your name
is
Gene right?

Daisy Days

I take my time in the morning
getting ready for a date by
putting sparkles on my skin and
combing my hair, so pleasantly
tulip-pink to match my flower print dress.
Boys in high school said dark skinned
girls like me can't be tulips, we're
thorns with dust bunny
hair so I'd take their girlfriends
for a ride and give them the bouquets
these boys wouldn't bother with.
Nowadays I can pucker up like
a spring time daisy, when I look in
the mirror and see the beauty of
dark cheeks, hair like the queens of legends,
and a lipstick smile just for the prettiest
dandelion.

The Piccadilly Sandwich Shoppe

I need the coins in my small silk
coin purse so I can buy each new dress,
straight off the racks in Harajuku,
straight off the runways of Paris,
straight into my dusty closet but I'm
sitting on a hill of student loans and
the only way to cut a tunnel through
lies in the piece of paper, an application
for lightning fast hoagie preparation
a block from my dormitory because
all the clothing shops are booked but
I'm so tired of last month's clothes and
I'm so tired of black hair roots and
Mama says I'm addicted to fashion but
I need the Benjamins because my favorite
brand just came out with a cute new
cupcake-print dress and pink dolly shoes,
(of which I only have four pairs).
I can put up with the mayonnaise smell
on my sleeves and late nights away from
my girlfriend; I can do it all for the
cupcake print.

Silver Dollar

Mustard stains are a normal part
of my day now.
Time seems hyperbolic, a
number that flies in and out the
window and doesn't stop to let
me offer some tea.
I'm working my way up these
ranks to fuel my unhealthy
addiction to fabrics tied together
while I don't even know where
life has gone. Home for the holidays
maybe? Even though it's only
late October and time is just
stopping in order to give me hours
to worry about my girlfriend,
who seems to be giving all of the
tea to Time. Time doesn't even
have a dollar to spare.

Lemon Squeeze

Babe's got night terrors and
I've got expired soup. We can both
be ugly together.

Except we're not ugly,
we're lightning strikes in meadows,
we're two empty bank accounts
(one robbed by cute dresses,
the other by alcohol)
and we're mice asleep on the carpet,
too scared to defy gravity in order to
get up and just land in bed.

She's sour and brittle, I'm
artificial sugar with grown-out roots.
I feel less delicate around her.

A Letter Sent Home

Dear Mom and Dad,
We're well into the first Semester,
and I'm on my last leg for ramen packets
and Capri Sun pouches.

I know I've had problems in the past
with over-spending on frills and lace,
imported dresses from Japan
and shoes straight from Paris,
but I work now. I make sandwiches
and wash dishes for those dresses.

My food account is running low,
soon I'll have to borrow from friends
or go hungry. I know I could use
money from work but there's this
BRIGHT PINK,
cosmic print dress and sometimes
I just have to sort priorities out,
you know?

Superstar

I'm going to be a designer someday,
so why do I have to be stuck in some
smelly sandwich shop anyway?
If only my boss could know just
who I am:

Reena Bateman, designer
of affordable and modern cute fashion,
available in an array of pastel colors
and sensible patterns.

I have a future as a superstar,
popping up on fashion blogs everywhere,
and I shouldn't have to bide my time
spreading mayonnaise on white bread
(or was it wheat they wanted? They
are asking for low-fat mayo, so probably.)

What I'll have to Say

New Year's is a few weeks away,
I head home tomorrow
without much to tell the folks.
Fashion marketing? It's going well!
The industry seems terrifying and
I have no clue just how I'll make
it when I'm up against the big names.
Relationships? I love my girlfriend, but
I hope for my future while both of you
fear it because artists can't bring
home the bacon, (most of them prefer
that tofu crap anyway) so why do I meddle
with them when I can get the premium-cut
business boys who will make millions some day?
Still a lesbian? I sure am and I don't
plan on adjusting. Next question, please.
What am I going to do with my life?
Funny you should ask because I'm not
even sure what I'm going to do tomorrow!

Alexander Rodriguez

Poison Kid

Draw me a line on the paper
ring it through ethernet portals
and bring me back to earth. I feel
the chill of old air conditioners and
rubbery mattresses. It's all grown familiar.
I can already see it, myself pounded
into this damn mattress three weeks from
now, a guy I have yet to know. I'm
here for today, a new day where I can
mold myself into something beautiful
through the pixels of the world wide
web and the thriving hell of outside
where I can show my scaly body and
glitter talons.

Frat Boys

College parties aren't like high school ones.
I mean for one thing, I'm invited.
I get to meet chiseled abs and square jaw
smiles on the most frustrating variety
of specimen known to gay mankind;
straight boys (AAAAH!)

I've got to say it's aggravating
when whiskey-breathed backwards hats
tug on your shirt before falling to the floor
and puking on some pair of stilettos
but no heaven-sent knight on a white horse
rides in to whisk you away to bed sheets
and wake up to kiss you on the forehead.

I need a boyfriend.

Giving him a name

I pour my heart out for the boy
at the club. Met him online
on dating sites where
pretty things like me go to breathe.
Let me leave behind
the hours of looking at the screen,
piling numbers on top of numbers
just so I can see him curve his body
around mine, compute the reality
of him coming home with me when
I still don't know his name yet but
he's beautiful, he's got curls like
a surfer and he can take me around
back, kiss me in the alley under the
blue lights projecting ratios into
my eyes, letting me see him and all
he's worked for even when I notice
the bruises on his chest.

Graffiti

I love the neon namesakes
sprayed onto the alleyways
outside the club where I talk to the
recipient of my kindergarten crush.
I love the feather boa
he places around my neck when
he calls me a pretty boy and promises
to talk to me after work. I sit out in
the dark (it's too crowded inside
and I don't like seeing him cooed
at like a baby doll) under the street
lights and the graffiti, wondering
if I'll one day have the balls to spill
my guts onto some brick wall and
tell that boy he deserves better than
nightclub bosses who make him sleep
with them for raises and belligerent
customers tripping him on account of
late liquor.

When You Fall Behind

When your books sit untouched
on your desk blanketed with dust,
and your computer screams
"Hey! I'm here too" from its
naked screen, you know that maybe
you have a problem. You haven't
checked your GPA in weeks-
perhaps it's on vacation while its
unsupervised cats tear up the house.
You're too busy programming a
trashy dream relationship to
give those cats a stern talking-to
or even go back to the coding and
calculations that manifested in your head
back in your bored adolescence (time
was your friend then and you didn't think
much for falling in love.)

Student Resource Baby

What number fell out of my eye
when I woke up on this couch here?
The cushion's got wispy lint crying out from
holes torn in red leather.
This room's got outside voices projected
from illusionary offices.
"Come in, Alexander."
Don't talk to me, I'm hungover.
Don't give me the daily grind.
2.0 is half of 4.0 but I think
they can still be friends. I forgot
what pencils look like. Luckily,
my knowledge of html is permanent,
I can't get rid of that even if I tried.
<item>
        <title>i'm a wasteoid</title>
</item>

How We Dance

Boys are useless under club lights,
am I even one of them?
How aggressively should I dance
while you're running around
serving itsy-bitsy teenie-weenie martinis
to stick-thin babes in tiaras?
Should I just sit out,
alone at one of the tables with drink stains,
where the backs of boys' heads are all I see.
Where are you going with that buff blonde?
Whose phone number is written on your hand?
Should we go dance when your shift ends?
Should I go home with you?
Or should I just sit here,
dancing in my head,
where you have time to stop and say hello.

Systematic Reflection

I look back on 8-bit years,
I'll be 19 in a few days so my
tattoos are nearly one year old,
my nose ring nearly three,
my venture out of the closet is
almost five. I've been programming
for six years now. I've been
crushing on this boy for about three months.
Without him, I still have years of me
to prove that I am a fabulous manifestation
of numbers and needles poked into me.
I am braver now than I was at fourteen,
and more decorated than ever
with scales inked along my neck and
gold in my skin.
I am a treasure trove,
I am real, and I enhance him with
my love, while his absence does not cost me.

Lila Mimoto

Scatterbrain

The moon woke me up at 3 am
and told me to grab a drink, finish
unpacking. Water the plants.
I didn't want to get ready yet,
and told the moon "Be quiet, I'm
trying my best." Tomorrow's just
another place to try, try, try.
I want to decorate the world someday,
but I want to stay practical,
land on my feet.
I want to live in the forest,
right now is time to fade into the
background of this industrial building,
throw my clothes off the hangers and
hide myself in the pile.
Tell my plants to eat my professors,
replace each figurehead with a Venus
fly trap. Lather, rinse, repeat.

Club Fair

Plastic tables fill the courtyard
with poster boards like neon lights
pulling me in by advertising knitting parties
like nightclubs and new bars across town,
though the faces here are friendlier.
"School Book Club", "Video Gaming Club"
none seem quite my niche
until I arrive at a small splotch of green
hidden in a crevice of the court yard
like a shiny penny in a shirt pocket.
"The Vegan Club: Saving the Environment
one Tofu Cube at a Time. Come to our
Garden-Planting Party on Tuesday 9/8 at
7:30 PM!" An androgynous individual with
impossibly shiny teeth hands me a flier.
"It's on Recycled Paper!" the person says.
I look at the poster board then back at the
club member. I stuff the leaflet in my pocket.
"I'll go," I think, *"But wouldn't the most
eco-friendly option just be to take a picture
of the details on the poster with my phone?"*

Leafy Greens

The Vegan Club holds its meetings
out on the grass of my dormitory's
courtyard, where our skin is pulled
at by gnats or cool air so that we may
condition ourselves in Mother Nature's
name and enjoy organic fruit juices,
cruelty-free. You might as well stamp
"cruelty-free" on all of your books because
it becomes a label for you as important
as a first name. This shampoo is cruelty-free,
not tested on the bunnies that run
through the same fields as the workers
slaving away over organic wheat but
I can't speak up because this is the
school vegan club and we need to go
remind the cafeteria workers that
meat is murder.

Grant the Ant

I fell asleep in English Lit
because my head became emotionally
attached to the book pile on my desk,
just as it does on several occasions,
which led me to have to rely on the only
other person I talk to in the vegan club,
a scrawny boy named Grant who likes
to talk to plants and wears bug-eye lenses
and screams bloody murder at most
intense social situations. He's trustworthy,
however, and being that he's in many of
my classes he's at least an ally in this
knock-on-wood world because he too
hates elitist vegans, but he too needs a friend.

Sickly

My name is Lila and I like
to run from the phone; there's
no time for a conversation. I'm going
sleepless til' the winter solstice.
I left papers on the desk for myself
but I never came in to get them.
Trapped in a dorm room with artificial
heat, the potted leaves above my bed are
shriveling up. Work doesn't get done
without Adderall, money doesn't get made
ever. I'm avoiding the vegan club due to an
unfortunate accidental whey incident.
I can't run anywhere, my legs have wilted
like the rest of me. I'm living alone in the
wilderness and writing papers for
Biology professors.

Where Friends Come From

I don't know how to live beyond gardens,
I don't know where to go to sleep
(simple answer: everywhere.
Pros: sleep
Cons: professors' snarky comments
become my alarm clock).
I can't make friends with vegans
who can recognize whey in pies on
the tips of their tongues.
I can't make friends with the other
girls living in my dorm building if
I still don't know their names.
I can't even figure out where friends
come from, other than the
garden section of the Hardware Store
or some kind old woman's small
botanical shop.

Parties

I'm not quite sure about this whole
college party deal. I went to
one under the stars, across the lake
where the fireflies picnic.
Some upper classmen had put
it together, told friends to invite
their friends who invited their friends,
and eventually word got to me.
Meanwhile, the closest friend I made there
was a drunk girl with blue fringe bangs who
came up and tried to compliment
my shirt before running to puke in
a trash can. It's really the thought that counts.
Don't know her name but she lives
on my floor and I got the joy of watching
her punch a senior in the face as
he tried to hit on her.
Don't know her story, either, but
at this point I still have yet to know
anyone's.

Shy Kid in the Commons

I haven't yet spent much of my time
away from the greenhouse that is my dorm
(that is of course when I'm not asleep
in a lecture hall of names I still don't know)
so when I introduced myself to the common room
where I got to watch a rather amusing
yet volatile war for the remote.
Among them I saw the girl with blue fringe bangs.
It wasn't long before she sat down with
the coveted device in hand.
She wasn't drunk or bruised or even irritated.
Instead, she started cuddling a pink-haired princess
to whom she handed the remote.
That girl, a recognizable face from my
English Literature course,
changed the channel to a reality show,
much to the dismay of the boys in the room.
Together, pink and blue, they sat on
their throne as queens of the commons.

A Bell of Novelty

Friends come better late than never,
more specifically right before I head home
to the forests of the Pacific north west
where trees reach for the sun and I
find solace in small cafes along the water.
But how can I ring in the New Year
when I'm busy wondering if Reena and
Gene will talk to me when I return?
Illinois is two hours ahead of Oregon
so by the time I go back I'll still be behind
with them ahead and knowing I'm old news,
a hanger-on who tricked herself into thinking
she'd have friends. I can dream of
new people to talk to as I start the next semester,
but the future still has to grow,
so I'll have to keep an eye on it.

Winter Break

December 19th – January 14th

Garret Marshall

Salisbury, North Carolina

Time and Sandwiches

This house is a quilt,
stitched together with old string and
pieces of hay. The patches are
sticky with old jam. Some are missing
because my parents are too busy
to sew new life into it. At least
I get to cook on my own. I've missed
making apple jam and bread,
spending hours over an oven that
doubles as a hearth. I'm a Southern
boy, a lover of the sweet and fried,
and a connoisseur of tradition.
But maybe time moves too slowly
when you're all alone down here.
You forget that you're wrapped in
a quilt, barely free to get up from
the couch.

Independent//Dependent

Well I spent about a half
hour with my parents over the
past three weeks. Business is money,
I know that much. College money,
transition money, retirement money,
good ol' Benjamins to get us through
the Winter and God, don't get me wrong,
I'm grateful but I still miss them
when I'm lighting the tree alone,
when I'm opening presents the next morning
(new sweater, socks, pants, apple jam to take
with me back to campus,)
when other relatives drop by but their questions
about my life don't mean as much as
Mom and Dad's.
I'm 18, dammit! I should be independent
but I've practically forgotten what Mom
and Dad look like. They couldn't even see me
off at the airport.

Gene Harper

Belleville, Illinois

Cough Syrup

The fire place is full of dust,
the fridge has a single package of
cheese, some milk, some apples.
This can only mean that Mom and Dad
are away, so the house feels like crumbs
at the bottom of a cookie jar.
I went down to the creek,
underneath the bridge where
graffiti covers like ivy and
sometimes a friend can be found
like an old sweater in the back of
the closet. Nobody was there today,
the town feels empty again and
my throat is starting to hurt.
I cough alone in my old bedroom.
Winter is the time of lonely
cough syrup-sipping.

Good Luck

Before I embark on the bus ride
back to whatever waits at Dodham,
I make sure to go back to the old Church,
really the classiest place in town
even though it's old as dirt. But I'm
not religious, I barely think of much beyond
the past and present, sure, but everyone mentions
that it's customary to say goodbye to
everyone before you leave and New Years
is the perfect time to refine yourself into a
less-rude amalgamation of life progression.
I walk along head stones, crunching
ice with my boots six feet above bones,
until I come to the last destination;
the plainest headstone I could imagine
ever bearing the date "February 22nd."
I leave a note, "Good Luck. To You
And To My Distress. May Both
Be Peacefully Dead."

Reena Bateman

Elizabeth, New Jersey

The Grace Period

I've really missed fire places.
There's something intrinsically wonderful
about sitting mere feet from a deadly heat,
because you're in a nice warm sweater
and cookies are in the oven. Your
family has stopped pestering you about school
and you're in the living room blocking
out Jersey frost with stress-free laying on the
carpet, cuddling with a fluffy calico friend.
I'm soaking it all in so I can think
of it all again during the pre-exam stress.
I finally got to re-dye my hair, bleach et al.
I get to look at all the dresses I left behind,
skirts too puffy for luggage
and blouses that I thought I'd never wear
but missed more than old friends.
Mom and Dad's judgment barely
crosses my mind while I'm sleeping in late.

Alexander Rodriguez

Orlando, Florida

Swamp Creature

Home, it's where the heat is,
down in Florida to wrap me up
and toast me to perfection. Clearly,
that's why I'm so great now. But
Florida and I have a love-hate relationship,
because I haven't heard from it
or its lovely residents, Mom and Pop,
for quite some time now. I can
use this as a chance to recover
from stressful midterms, but when I
stumble off this plane I will be one
with 75 degrees again, and thank God
reptiles have cold blood,
so they adapt to their surrounding
temperatures. Ma was never too
fond of reptiles, and maybe that's
why she never bothered to call.
After all, we aren't very soft,
and we're too slimy for the more
squeamish of Floridians, those sensitive
to abnormalities.

And Home Feels Like...

I actually have no clue
what it feels like honestly, I
hopped off the plane and crashed
into bed. Now I've been
home for two weeks and it's still
mostly been sleeping and working
on the computer in order to get
back into the swing of assignments
before I forget how to do basic html.
I don't remember much of friends
down here in The Sunshine State
and Mom and Dad have other relatives
over, so they're busy gushing over
the guests who aren't me. I think
the most work and sleep I've gotten
done this entire academic year has been
in this very bedroom at my folks' house.

Lila Mimoto

Newport, Oregon

Slap Us on a Christmas Card

Being home for the holidays
is basically the same as being
stuck in the airport. Tons of people
have come in from all over the place
and many of them don't speak English
particularly well. That's the case for
Aunt Mia and Uncle Koto on
my dad's side, immigrants
from Japan to France who decided to fly
over to Oregon for the holidays and speak
fluent Japanese and French, but English is
a challenge. Same with Grandma Ruth
and Grandpa David, my Mom's parents who flew
in from Israel for the holidays, even though
Hanukkah was three weeks ago. Plus, there's
cousin Ben, who brought his wife Sophia
from Germany, though ironically she
speaks better English than he does.
Still, me being here is hardly anything
special, not when all these esteemed
guests have dropped by.

Spring Semester

January 15th – May 20th

Garret Marshall

The End Goal

So I arrive back at campus,
bundled up in a new sweater,
ready for whatever the hell gets
thrown at me for the Spring semester.
Check my bank account like the
money-conscious young adult that I am
and there, in all of its 4-digit glory,
is a brand new deposit. "Total Amount:
$9,046." I stand there, like this is some
cruel dream or whatever, blinking to wake up
like a cartoon character. The numbers
don't go away. They, instead, sit
at approximately $6,000 more than
what had been in my account last week.
In my messages, a single unread string
of words beckons to me. "Hope you saw
our little late gift. Sorry we couldn't see you
off. G-pa and G-ma chipped in so make sure
to tell them you love them. We can
help you set up a surgery date when
you're ready. Love, Mom
and Pop."

Quitters

I threw in the towel today.
Boss Man told me I was too moody
and temperamental and if I kept on this
way, I'd get fired. Good thing I threw the
first punch. Literally. I punched a wall
a few days ago and severely screwed my hand.
Oh well, at least I refused to sit around
like a sitting duck ready to get fired.
I mean I have the money for top surgery
and I got sick of being stuck serving
breakfast to ungratefuls while I could
be doing just about anything else.
I chose a surgery date, I can get my
grades up, I can talk to my friends,
I can get it together because I deserve happiness.
Speaking of happiness, guess whose
now ex-boss signed him up for group therapy?
Yeah, I'll show up to that. Totally.

Showing Up

We were tense and small people
strung into a circle and since I hate
feeling tense and small I wanted
to up and leave but-
"Hi, and your name is…?"
Great. They all know I'm here and
"I'm Garret" and "I'm a cooking major"
and "I don't know why I'm here."
Sure they would notice if I left
and sure someone in the group would
talk to me eventually because I know
some of them. There's Liz and Brit and
Eric and this girl who I think is named
Gene and that's about it but it's enough to
be sketchy if I leave and I'm just
going to listen to everybody else's sob story
to distract from my own problems or something.
Cool. We all grabbed magic markers and
nametags from a bin passed around.
"Garret" in plain letters covered
the pocket of my flannel. My only thought
was "Great, now I've been branded and
I won't ever be allowed to leave.

Ripple

There is a ripple in my progression
and it calls from across the circle.
In fact, the caller is none other than
the Group Counselor, who along
with myself, makes a perfect diameter
of about fifteen feet in the middle of our
circle.
"So Garret, I know you said you don't know
why you're here, but do you have any guesses
why you were referred?"
Well yeah, I'm an angry transgender kid has issues
accepting that The World Isn't Fair, so of course
someone would look at me and go "hey, there's
a real piece of work if I've ever seen one," but
I'm not gonna tell Mr. Hippie Counselor Guy
since I don't wanna be the designated kid
with the anger issues so instead I spat an
"Beats me. I guess I didn't make the
best impression at work." Somewhere
adjacent to me, I could feel Gene making
a face of ironic judgment. It wasn't cruel by
any means, since us angry people have to
stick together.

Well That Sure Was A Load Off My Chest

Yesterday, I spent $6,000 to have
globs of fat removed from my chest.
It's far more satisfying than it sounds.
I'm wearing a big ol' bandage wrap
spitting out tubes that drain into
these plastic doggy bags and I couldn't
be happier. It hurts like a bitch
but now I won't have to scramble for
my chest binder anymore
and loosen, now tighten, now loosen,
take a DEEEEEEP breath, tighten,
loosen, don't crack those ribs.
Now I can breathe like other boys do.
My parents have brought me ice water
and soup and I haven't brought myself
to grab it, even after they left.
I'm not paralyzed, just sore, lying down
as the stubble on my chin grows by the second
and my torso feels infinitely more weightless.

Finalize

My chest is healing and I'm
almost bandage-free. I take my finals
in three weeks. I'm eating breakfast
back in shitty Gingham with a girl from
my counseling session named Gene,
her girlfriend, and my good friend Lila.
Gene wondered how the hell we knew each
other and I felt bad that I had no better answer
than the truth- a psychology presentation
that we got a C on. It went surprisingly well
considering our polar personalities and
conjoined lack of work ethic.
Oh well, school's almost done anyway
and then I get to go home and cook.
It's almost Vidalia onion pie season.
Pie season in general is a time for some star power.
Maybe I can make a halfway decent job
out of it this summer.

Narrow

I have a sneaking suspicion that
I'm going to need group counseling
next year. I'm realizing that the
time I blew up at a kid and stabbed him
with a pencil in second grade, the time
I got pulled over for chasing a cop car
because he cut me off, the time
in high school that I chopped
ALL (and I do mean every single one) of the
vegetables in our house into teeny tiny bits
because my teachers refused to call me
Garett and insisted on my birth name-
all of those are indicative that bad tempers
can basically manifest in the womb. I'm
not going to magically chill out this summer.
I'm not done sitting in circles and introducing myself
and talking about how my week went.
Things are looking up but I'm not done,
not by a long shot.

Gene Harper

With That, We Dance

With a crowded court yard,
snow cushions on untouched benches,
a hidden room with four dark corners
and a bed where we can hide under the covers,
kisses that keep our lips from freezing,
friends who share café pizza,
rips in my uncle's old leather jacket,
nights spent awake with black coffee,
snack cakes bought at 2am, eaten at 2:30 am,
(neither you nor me nor Lila could sleep),
movies until sunrise, makeup-less mornings,
bathrooms that smell like cinnamon and
someone's burning hair, flat-iron still plugged in,
thrift store blankets, sweaters we steal from each other,
we dance with them all.
You knew I loved winter when you fell in love with me,
and so, frost-bitten, we dance and we dance.

Five Helpful Tips for Dying your Hair

1. Forget that you have a natural hair color.
   Forget that you existed in a state prior to that
   of your current self. Forget how much
   bleach stings your forehead.

2. Section off your bangs from the rest
   of your hair. Grab the bleach. Grab
   the electric blue. Grab an old t-shirt
   Get ready for a chemistry experiment on your scalp.

3. You're sitting on your bed
   waiting for your hair follicles to
   finish burning. Call your girlfriend,
   eat a hot pocket, draw the porcupine
   that you feel is bashing into your
   head. Don't think too hard, it stresses out
   the hair follicles and then they won't burn fast enough.

4. Shower time. Don't be alarmed by how
   tired your hair feels. You're tired too, you can't judge.
   Get out, towel dry, you're ready for electric blue.
   It's supposed to be the color of a lightning storm,
   but instead it's the color that you wanted your future
   boyfriend's car to be when you were 10. Now you're a
   lesbian and it's the color all over your hands.

5. Finish off by retouching the black
   that you sectioned off from the bangs. The
   girl on the box of dye looks like Cleopatra.
   You look like a bruise. Let yourself think that you got the
   better deal.

Mr. Pig Meat

He's there like he always is,
the boy who hands out bacon and
sausage down in Gingham. Curly
hair is locked onto his head and
a baseball cap is keeping it safe. He
looks bored. Nametag reads "Garrett"
pinned to a tan polo.
He knows now not to ask
me "Bacon or Sausage?" because he
knows I'm not the biggest fan of pig meat.
He looks bored but he remembers. Sometimes
I wish he would ask me again, because
he has a charming Southern accent and
maybe one day when he's on break
I might want to sit down and talk to
him and let him know that he doesn't have
to be the bored pig meat guy. That's ridiculous,
though, because he's a stranger and so am I,
and I don't want to distract him from the
work of neatly placing sausage links on
plates.

Rubbernecking

February came to me, swollen,
beating at my window with sleet
and trying to kill me when I didn't
say hello. I slipped and fell on the way
to class. Not too bad, but the back of
my upper left thigh is covered in bruises
and I'm sore all over. Sounds about right.
I can look back at our past years. Last year
was the 22nd when he killed himself, the year before
I was claws deep in trying to breathe on
my own while my parents fought and Mom
was threatening to leave with me up to
Canada or Minnesota or Washington state
because they were all warmer than my dad's
heart or something like that. By then,
I just wanted to be on my own. The year
before, Illinois saw its worst blizzard on record
and I was locked in the house with them bickering
over how to pay for heat. Every year was more
depressing than the last, and I look back
on them dumbfounded, wondering why
this is the time that people like to focus
on being in love.

Angry People

I saw Garrett, the "Bacon or
Sausage?" Southern-fried bored guy
doing what he does best: look incredibly
underwhelmed while serving breakfast.
I saw him punch a wall outside the restrooms
after breakfast hours has ended. He fell
into himself, with his hands atop his head
as he pulled his curls, now free of their
baseball cap prison.
I saw him look up, realize the small
crack that he had made in that wall and then
glance side to side to see if anyone had noticed.
He sighed and turned around, only to find
me staring.
"You okay, dude?"
"Work sucks. And walls. They suck too."
"You should quit. Find somewhere that
doesn't suck."
"Wish it were that easy. Capitalism sucks."
Can't say I remember what I said next,
so maybe now I'll have the audacity to
discuss it with him over coffee next time.
We, the angriest of people, need to look out for
each other.

Ignite

I fill my flask with fire,
I'm a walking Molotov cocktail,
sipping poison gas and letting my
lungs fly. But who am I kidding,
I'm a drunk exclamation point,
passionate and tipsy-topsy, throwing
commas everywhere because I can
never just cut to the chase. I'm an
exclamatory alcoholic, drinking because
I'm bored and a high BAC makes me
more passionate and I can messily kick
and punch at boys throwing themselves out
windows to try and get my number.
But when I overhear kids talking shit about
alcoholics grinding their lives away with
every pop of a bottle cap, I sit back and
wonder why I turn to Molotov cocktails
when I have the sensitivity of a grenade
and the blast power of a pipe bomb when
I'm lying in bed trying to figure out
what the fuck is going on beyond
counting down days, since
February's in double digits now.

Go Off

We all know what today is, it
says it right on our phone screens. Thursday,
February 22nd. 9:00 AM. I have a 10:30 Psych
lecture. I use Jack Daniel's as mouthwash. I
don't change out of my pj's. I get back
under the covers and barely move. I check
my phone.
"You can do this babe! Distract yourself. Come
to breakfast." Thanks Reena. Not sure how
well that will go when
"*If only anyone bothered. Believe me, I asked.*"
keeps coming back up.
"*My friends all have better things to do.*"
Stop.
"*I was in love with her and she didn't love me back
and I thought I was okay with that. Guess not. She
can move on and I won't be hurt now.*"
STOP.
"*There's not much else I can do now. Not here.*"
FUCKING STOP DON'T DO THIS.
There's a knock at my door.

Debris

Lila wrapped her arms around my
torso. My head wasn't up to figuring
out what was going on.
"Reena and I are worried. You didn't
respond to her text even though it said
you saw it and it's been 45 minutes."
"That's nothing. Don't worry"
"Gene, please." I looked up to see Reena
behind her, paper bag in hand.
"Croissants. Are you going to class today?"
"I know I should, at least. Thanks."
Gingham makes some mean croissants.
I wonder if Garret helped to make them.
Pause.
"I tried my best."
"We can walk with you there."
"I don't know if I'm going."
*"You can find me in the river,
if you bother to look."*
"We can stay here with you if you want.
Will Ashlyn mind?" Ashlyn is my room mate.
Reena is my girlfriend. Lila is an angel of
a best friend. Today is February 22nd and
I'm alive.

"She went to class already. You guys
can stay. I'll go to my later classes."
We watched film noir on my laptop
and I laid against them.

Rip Ya' Tights

Hi, my name is Gene and I'm a fuck-up.
.....Hi Gene...
I like to rip my tights when I get nervous
and right now there's a big ol' hole along
my thigh.
The whole prospect of group therapy makes me nervous.
I'm still nervous. Even if you try to appease my nerves and
tell me it will get easier, it's still going to make me nervous.
I'm still here though.
It's a toss-up as to whether or not I slept last night.
The last two nights. Three.
There's a 99% chance this is all in my head,
and I'm sitting here silently through group
therapy while everyone else introduces themselves.
There's a 1% chance I'm saying this all out loud
and I'm already making the BEST worst first impression.
Oh well, fight me.
There is quiet. Someone else's mouth is moving.
You can't hear it. Way to go, Gene. You're crazy.
I need to take my multi-vitamin when I get back.
I'm not sure I ate earlier.
There's a big hole in my knee.
There's a big hole running the back of my thigh.
Nobody else's mouth is moving right now.
Oh.
It's actually my turn to talk.

I for I

I give up my eye so that I may hear,
I give up my ears so that I may taste,
I give up my mouth so that I may look
onto reimagined fields of view without
them taking my breath away.

I give up my old self for I,
Me-oh-my, I, I, I,
I am not defined by friends under bridges and
Southern Illinois summers with rusted fences
and I can give up on my recollection of them in the present,
because they are not my present.
I give them up for the present I.

I, who dyes my hair because I exist how I want to exist.
I, who falls in love while laying in the court yard
with a pink-haired princess.
I, who defends the self with self defense, along
the lines of punching in parabolas
((lower the arm, ball the fist, raise to his chest))
when a boy gets too close and I've had too much to drink.
I, who learns of angry café workers, befriends tired vegans,
and is accustomed to loving everyone but herself.

I give up the "I" that is accustomed. I trade it for the "I"
that is adapting.

Minnow

At the group session they told me
I was depressed because I focus my efforts
only on art. So I decided to show them
what I accomplish without art.
Specifically by writing a shitty song for Reena,
googling the genetic makeup of lettuce,
putting stars in my agenda next to papers
that were due two weeks ago and I still need
to write. I downloaded 50 live versions of Tom
Jones' "It's Not Unusual" and played them
all to Reena over the phone. I went over
to her dorm and tried on a bunch of her frilly dresses
and felt like a god damn princess because I forgot
what expensive clothes felt like.
And the whole time I knew what I felt like,
a silly little minnow in a pond of talents
and I don't know what to do but sit
around and draw while the world
innovates without me.
I need to update my therapy group on this.

I Am So Tired and Full of Rage

Consider this what college is all about.
We aren't consciously "finding ourselves
and our soul mates and the knowledge we
need to change the world." We're sitting
around in the dorm commons, hung-over,
eating stale chips, and wondering
how to make money when you can't work
and your bank account is empty.
We are mentally cursing the traditions of
American Higher Education, we are wearing
Our student loans on our sleeves.
We are getting sick every month because
illnesses spread faster in dorm halls,
we are staining shared bathrooms with
hair dye and rushing to clean it up.
We are starving ourselves when the dining hall
closes too early and we're out of food at the dorm.
We can't romanticize the lives we're living
right now, so maybe we will 10 or 20 or 30 years
from now but in the meantime we're
sitting in lecture halls playing games online
instead of taking notes for class.

Confiscated

Yeah, yeah, way to go
at whoever decided to send in
the complaint about me drinking
in the dorm building. Ashlyn was
it your idea? You're not even here
half the time you're usually off with some
boy but now I'm on some kind of weird
~probation~ where if I get caught again
I'll lose my guaranteed housing for next year
but right now the school is going to make me
continue group therapy along with one-on-one
and of course my parents have been contacted
so of course they're cutting off my funds
for the next month. In summary,
thanks a lot to whichever god damn snitch
it was who looked at me and thought
"Gee damn! I might as well tell Administration
about that drunk girl with the blue hair even though
EVERYBODY is sneaking alcohol into the dorms,
am I right or am I right?"

Bathing in Wine

Reena and I have been dating for
eight months (somehow???)
and when I woke up to find
bath soaps, art pens, new shorts
(she claims I don't dress summery enough)
I was suspended in disbelief.
Love affairs always fell out of fashion with me
after you gave it a couple weeks.
But apparently I've given Reena eight months.
At this point she feels less like a girlfriend,
more like a close friend that I can kiss,
more like someone who won't go out of style.

One of my bath products turns the water
red like wine and it smells like oranges and spice.
The shorts have tiny tears over the pockets.
The markers are all pastel in color.
Reena is making our future more glamorous.

Atoms

The atoms in my head are dancing with ideas-
they can't decide whether I deserve to be here
with Reena or not.
What I did was despicable
                but I deserve a warm bed, cute girlfriend.
But he killed himself over me
                even though I didn't tell him to do that.
He never finished high school
                and that was his choice not mine.
I could kill myself now
                but my choices can be different from his.

The atoms in my head can't sleep
but the atoms in my arms let me wrap around Reena at night
and the atoms in my legs let me carry all this weight
for all of these days I've got left.

Expressive

I wore blue velvet
and love can be ours.
When I go back to Illinois in three days,
I will still remember east coast water,
hazy sunsets, creaking boardwalks,
elastic with waterlogged wooden veins.
I will hold them all in my pocket
and spark them out when I need inspiration.
When I am 90 and my bones creak like that
same worn boardwalk,
I will still be an artist,
because I will have what I've seen now.
The pictures will spend eons blending into one another
like the reds and oranges of the Sun saying goodnight.
Before it goes to bed I can thank it for making me expressive.
I will thank Reena for the color pink,
because now it belongs to her.
I will thank this calendar for moving me forward
instead of stopping me in my tracks.

Reena Bateman

Wait What?

I got a 95 on my Fashion Marketing midterm,
A 97 on my English Literature midterm,
A 93 on Statistics,
a 98 in Foundations of Art,
92 in macro-Biology,
and I made the Dean's List?
How does that even work, how
do I go from a painfully average high school
student to actually making something
of myself in college? Naturally I worked
my butt off, but I had no clue I would
do so well. Take that Mom and Dad, your
baby girl is working her way up! Take that,
to all the kids and teachers in high school
who over-looked me because I was a black girl
with an affinity for unnatural hair colors
and drawing in the middle of class!
Take that, to everyone who ever thought I wasn't
going to ever know what to make of myself!

Live from your Local Lecture Hall

Asleep when I should be awake,
of course that's why they keep the lights
so bright, but maybe when I sit far enough
back, the professors won't notice that I'm
using their tables as pillows. What would
I tell them if they asked? I'm pulling
A's in their classes, I'm just spending a
little too much time with a night owl
of a girlfriend and another friend who can
basically fall asleep anywhere. "Well,
they don't sound like the best influences,"
believe me my parents have told me all
that much. "You can't have a successful
career while you're busy dragging slackers around,"
Well maybe I care about those slackers enough
to keep them by my side. "Well what if they're
just going to feed off you for the rest of your life?"
Well, I know enough about myself to not
let that happen, right? Don't I?

The Mom Friend

Has anyone ever noticed how
every group of friends has a designated
responsible one who protects the other
friends and makes sure that they don't
do stupid things? I think that friend is me.
Once high school ended and I had my
weird shift from Angsty Teenager to
Future-Oriented Young Adult, I also
started dating an emotional alcohol-abuser
with a knack for threatening to fight people
at parties, and I befriended a sweet but lazy
narcoleptic who lacks any and all motivation
beyond raising a successful garden.
Some of their friends (who are magically
my friends somehow) are not too different,
so I strap them in and drive them around
everywhere and make sure they know how
to be polite to others. I basically make sure they
don't get scraped up too bad and
I fix their cereal in the mornings and I put bandages
on scraped knee caps and I read bedtime stories.
I wonder how much they notice?

Pretty Pity

There's a pretty boy who compliments me
often enough that it keeps me from not noticing him.
He's tattooed to look reptilian and the tunnels in his
earlobes are 1,000x the size of regular ear piercings.
I bet they could hold small mice.
I bet he would like that since the inked scales on his neck
look like those of a snake. He wears a backwards hat
and baggy clothing. He looks tired, and
aggressive when he's not mid-flattery.
Not that he's mean, because a mean person wouldn't
compliment my dresses every couple of days.
Mean people don't take time out of their days
to smile and say your hair looks nice.
I don't know if he exists anywhere else on this
campus besides the common area of my dorm building.
I wonder what he does.
I wonder if I know how to talk to people I don't know,
I wonder if he thinks he's pretty, because
I think he's pretty. He looks like a polar opposite
to compliment me, and I commend anyone
who's talented enough to do that.
I think I would like to do his makeup.

Ugly Spring

Spring Break is almost here and you know what that means.
It means that this place should be prettier than it is.
What the heck, Dodham?
Where are the blooming hydrangeas?
The sunshine that hugs like cashmere sweaters?
I'd even take the dandelions that interrupt the
monotony of boring old grass, but no.
All we're getting right now is a cold rainy season
to comb over the dirty slush of snow from the winter.
It's mid-March and I have yet to see any of it.
They say Jersey's ugly, but home has nothing on
the upset of Illinois right now.
Going out in my dresses and mary-janes would be a waste.
I'd dare say that this weather is only
Sweatpants-appropriate. (Gasp!)
But I still maintain my standards somewhat and
bother to show up to class in a blouse and some nice jeans.

Baby Brown Eyes

From the black roots of my hair,
to the tips of my tiny tiny toes,
I am a goddess.
With my faded pink hair,
city of split ends,
pink eye shadow fading and creasing,
nose too big for my face,
I am flawless.
I dress myself in hundreds of dollars,
pretty pastel cupcake factory prints on jumper skirts
in the biggest size available from that line
thanks to teeny weeny Japanese brands.
I straighten my hair and then curl it
because I'm redundant and I have time to do so
because I'm a morning person.
I buy like a Kardashian on a shopping spree,
I ask for more money like a kid in a candy store,
I work my ass off to get by.
I love myself, with my baby brown eyes,
hourglass body, and bark brown skin
tied up in polka dot bows.
I was able to carry it all for a year's worth.

Jersey Summer

Gene is coming home with me
at the end of the semester for a few weeks.
Her parents gave us the okay,
mine gave us a shifty 'alright.'
She'll get to see Jersey sand in 90 degrees.
I'm praying she won't drink herself into a coma
with the other college kids stopping by the shore.
I keep telling her she's not going to run into guidos,
I swear there aren't that many guidos.
What I haven't told her is that I
I hope the summer loves us.
I hope I can win her a prize at the boardwalk
and get a summer job so I can buy some new wigs,
new makeup, new dresses.
I hope Mom and Dad fall in love with her
when they meet her.

If I get any work done it will be a God send.
If I can find myself creating again,
find artistic inspiration in a Jersey summer,
I will renounce my atheism.

Embark

Lila went to the airport with us,
hugged us 'til we had to board.
I don't know why but I think I saw her crying.

On the plane I started a summer art journal.
I hadn't done a journal since high school.
5 seconds into it I cut my finger on a tape dispenser
and Gene laughed at me.

I had no trouble finding my luggage when we hit Jersey.
It was a set of big bright pink suitcases and
when it came around, everyone at the gate stared at me.
I hadn't even worn anything that spectacular
and a little girl asked if I was a princess.

Gene and I took a cab to my house
and when my parents saw her, they shook her hand
and complimented how tall she was.
But did they realize how cute her laugh is?
Can they see all of our inside jokes woven
between our fingers when we hold hands?
They'll pick up on it someday.

Alexander Rodriguez

Freaking

Well shit. You see, you don't
really hear much about the kids who
did well in high school but proceeded
to drop off the face of the earth afterwards.
I can tell you right now that I'm living their
stories out with each passing day.
Naturally, when you're busy working on
computer programming and math problems
instead of experimenting with all the bullshit
you want to try, you're gonna be an Honor Roll
Sweetheart, but once college comes along
and you're let out of the cage,
all the grades start to spiral down,
down,
down,
until you look like a hung-over freak
when you go to check your scores
and you shift in your pajama pants as you
read off "C, D, F, F, D, C…." for midterms.

Wowzers

In taking a break from night club adventures,
I find myself not working on school work,
no, but sitting around playing video games
and contemplating the binding ways of gender.
It's like productivity is allergic to me
and decides to go run with my friends instead.
Speaking of that whole gender identity thing,
What The Hell Is This?
Maybe I'm not a boy, because what the hell
even are boys? But girls possess a certain
grace that I lack and I could never be
that graceful. Maybe I'm something
far more cryptic and maybe I just
do not know. All I do know is I just
pirated five new games and I can toggle
with the programming to relieve any tension.

Isms

I anger with grade point idealism
studying contextualism for English,
capitalism and communism and why they matter
and why my history professor believes in authoritarianism
and I brush toward anarchism, freedom of the students,
freedom of the people, true egalitarianism.
But when the footfalls of your college career are rooted in
expressionism rather than internalism in what I have learned,
and I dabble in irrationalism by escaping to clubs with boys,
lose myself in mysticism when I look in a mirror and know
I can do more. I can do better. Perfectionism.
Cover my face in makeup, an extreme form of feminism.
Cover myself in tattoos for all sense of individualism.
I should cut myself from materialism, making me
look like I practice libertarianism when I fall
more toward Marxism. I think about the road ahead,
a sort of spiritualism of heavens ahead,
like reaching Nirvana in Buddhism, and I think
I'm not sure if college is all that right for me.

Le Pauvre

Hello, yes, Mom and Dad?
I know you guys want me to become
a computer engineer but, consider,
I am a diva, I am made of fishnets and lipstick,
I'm too scary-looking to hire in an office.
The fact that I know how to program is a bonus,
it is not my defining factor and I'll have you know
that I'm fine being a doll face in debt
than a scatterbrained mess somewhere with
more logical people. I know this sounds
edgy and cliché (sorry guys) but wait I don't
need to apologize to anyone because my life
belongs to me only and I don't need to care
and I am real and I will thrive and I'm
considering dropping out.
School has drowned me for years now and
this year I thought that I had hit rock bottom,
but really I learned how to swim away.

The Cause of the Deadbeats

Florida is already sweating in March
I mean I come home from shitty fake Spring in Illinois
to Florida, the armpit of America.
But at this point I know that I'll spend this time
finding the tacky island-themed bars that will let me drink,
finding other cute college gay guys here to visit,
since my time with that boy back home is no-strings attached
and I haven't even seen him for a few weeks.
I'm trying not to care.
I'm trying to figure out how my parents feel about me
dropping Dodham, toying with gender,
tying myself up in a pretty little bow.
I'm 19 and my own person but damn I'd be lying if
I said I wanted them to stop giving me any funds.
I'd be lying if I said I wasn't afraid that I'm one of the
only kids doing this shit.
Maybe I can be a martyr for the kids who'd been too scared
to leave and felt too forced into the idea that you have to
go to high school,
college,
professional work.
So when I go up to those gay boys here for the week
I can say kiss me, I'm a deadbeat.

On Gap Years

Shockingly enough, I'm listening
to my mother's advice. She tells me
not to drop college all together and
here I am, not dropping college all
together. Instead I'm taking a year
and I'm going to go into the city
and maybe try to find some cute little
job while I ask if I want to go back.
Maybe not to Dodham but somewhere else.
Somewhere where the summers last forever
(shirtless guys, always a plus)
and I can expand beyond programming
into every other little glass piece
that makes up the mosaic of whatever the hell
I feel like doing. I'm writing out ways that
I can go to Administration and tell them
that I'm going to be gone next year.
To them, I'm probably just 1 out of 6,034.
They probably won't miss me much.

Why I picked Dodham // Why I'm Leaving Dodham

My name is Alexander Rodriguez,
Shawton High Class of 2015
and I'm selecting Dodham University
in Illinois, where I will major in Computer Science.
Dodham seems like the right school for me,
because it is affordable at $25,000 per year,
accepts 94% of applicants,
and has a large LGBT population for students like me.

My name is Alexander Rodriguez,
former Dodham University freshman,
class of 2019. I'm selecting to take a gap year
here in Florida, where I will find a job
somewhere in Orlando and I will decide what
I want to do. I'm a member of the class of ????
I'm figuring out just what my identity is,
and I can do it on my own, without a dorm room,
a lecture hall, and residents of the state of Illinois.

The Call of the Slackers

You aren't allowed to forget about
students like me. Some say we fade
into the back rows of classrooms,
get our subpar grades, graduate in
the lower half of our class and smile faintly
in group photos.

I refuse to let you forget me,
because I spent nights on the verge of tears
as I stared blankly at my computer screen,
no will to write.

You can not forget every time that
I fell asleep in a lecture hall and everyone
laughed when the professor made some snarky
comment to wake me up and I called him an asshole
under my breath because I was embarrassed.

I'll make it impossible to forget me,
when I change the world and you see
me as more than some kid showing up ten minutes late.

Students like us do great things every day,
like continuing to get out of bed.

Lila Mimoto

Crowded

I forgot that being at home
was just as busy and boisterous
as the college campus. I forgot
that sneaking off to gardens and
beachside cafes just summoned wails
from a relative, "LILA! GET BACK HERE!
WE'RE CARVING THE TURKEY!"
Imagine it in your best angry-Israeli voice.
It takes a lot of patience to be an
introvert in a big family and by the
time the last of that energy is burned away,
college slaps you with a wake-up call
(literally- I'm back to 8 AM again)
and says "HEY! 25,000 PEOPLE
LIVE HERE! HAVE FUN,"
so maybe I will have to lose all
two of the friends I made here because
I just want to hide in my dorm
until I can exist in society again.

Pow

Ironically, I have found my comfort
in the midnight adventures with friends,
watching old movies on laptops
and eating donuts with frosted sugar
that sticks to you like paste.
Moronically, I have lost sleep in
these nights and as a proud
sleep-connoisseur, I can't say this has
the best effect on my class performance.
Chronically, I feel like not just a third
wheel but a spare tire hugging onto
the back of a Jeep for dear life
because it can't bear the thought
of being alone, even if the other wheels
are perfectly fine on their own right
now and that spare is just not needed.
Neurotically, I wonder if I am a good fit,
if I am doing what's best, if I am
getting enough nutrients from a vegan diet,
if I am a firecracker all set to explode.

Current

The branches won't stop dancing
and when a storm comes up on this Oregon shore
I will melt away with the waves.
I don't know if I'm going to meet land,
but I hate the idea of going back anywhere.
My friend, a charmer from North Carolina,
told me that I'm one of the only safe people
because I'm always asleep, happy, or lost in thought.
I'm lost in saltwater.
Southern boys are always charmers or they're evangelicals,
there never seems to be a middle ground
but I'm lucky he's the former.
But good friends don't amount to a future in anything,
and I'm still undeclared in just about everything.
But I do know if too much saltwater fills my pores,
I'll swell up like a cork in a bottle lost at sea.

Noodles for Breakfast

I woke up to find Gene on my couch in an old t-shirt
eating leftover Chinese food. It's still strange to
consider that I actually brought a friend home
with me for spring break and some times I have
to double-blink just to make sure she's really there.
She said that her house was too small to hold all her baggage
and her town was too lonely for her
so I brought her with me here to Oregon. My extended family's
constant plane travels had earned us a buy-one-get-one-free deal.
We stay up all night watching cheesy 80's movies,
slurping noodles out of chopsticks,
zipping up our hoodies and walking in the rain.
To think I would have other friends to accompany us if they
could afford the flights. To think that even when my
motivation's in the mud, there are others there with me
as if we're in a cutely pathetic motivation mud-bath.
To think that I can walk along rough sandy shores
with my best friend in comfortable silence.
It's as comforting as Pacific Northwest mist.

Daily Double

When I was little,
my mother always called me a *luftmensch*
because that's what her father called her brother
when he ran around pretending to fly.
She told me it meant that I was an airhead,
that I didn't know what I was doing,
that I couldn't think much.
It wasn't until yesterday that I learned
that *luftmensch* means "air man" in German,
"dreamer" in the Yiddish context. At Passover,
when my *saba* from Israel asked how I was
doing in college, he called me a real air man,
a real dreamer, for wanting to make a greener Earth
through botany. My mother told him to have more
faith in his granddaughter. He told her that
no, no, he is *proud* and he sees me doing
great things if I keep reaching high enough.
That night, Gene told me she thinks I have more
potential than her and I can't give up on anything,
not just yet, not when I've got so much left to do.

Better Off

Am I better off than I was a year ago?
My hair is the same length,
I still don't want to grow it out
or re-dye it for that matter.
Brown ends with black roots is not
that bad of a look.
I'm still the same height, a sad 5'2"
and I still tell everyone to be gentle with me.
The only difference is that I'm 365 days older
and I have 30 college credits.
And I have new friends
and I have to take a plane to get home
and I have to give all my plants to Gene
so I don't have to find out how to get them through TSA.
Maybe I am better off.
Who knows, I'm thinking about this while
wandering around lost in the airport.
My perception hasn't gotten any better and
I still fall asleep when I'm not supposed to,
that much I do know.

K.I.T.

Don't throw me away like tights
with a hole in the crotch
(scratch that, Gene, I bet you'd still wear them)
and don't scratch me off nail polish
when you're bored in class
(I saw you doing it Reena, don't deny it.)
I don't have friends back in Oregon and
you guys are half a country, a country,
a countless string of miles in thousands away.
Skype can join our friend group for the months to come.
And while you talk to your old friends
I'll be sleeping in Pacific northwest mist,
trying to understand languages I don't speak
(thanks to the mixing pot of family relations)
and I'll be growing friends
in little ceramic pots on my windowsill.
They won't talk as much as you guys do.

Breathers

Self esteem may not be my forte
but I am proud of myself,
I am proud that I made it through
A WHOLE YEAR OF COLLEGE
and I am proud that I started using my voice
and making myself stay awake longer.
I am drinking more water every day,
I am spending more time drawing,
I am talking,
I am thriving.
I can let this summer be a breather,
because I know that I will have friends in the fall
and I can make friends right now.
I can go apply for a job at the fresh market.
I can write a self-help book.
I can get a tattoo.
I'm 18 going on 19 and I am
Breathing, breathing, breathing.

Acknowledgements:

I exist without exploding because of these lovely individuals:

Kaylee Chapman, my wonderful cover artist and best friend. Without you, this book would not be nearly as fashionable. When I inevitably take over the world, I'm looking forward to you being my right hand man. Daniele, my best friend and the number one person to go on adventures with when I want to distract myself from words and look at people instead. Hayley, who made it through this all before and always reminded me that I could do this. Thank you for your words, your hugs, and your puns.

The Lit Class of 2016. Thank you for the best of support and the harshest of critiques when I needed both. The future will send us thousands of miles apart, so I hope many of you know that I'm a pencil, some paper, and a stamp away.

Mrs. Supplee and Mrs. Tenly, who somehow managed to put up with me on a daily basis. Thank you for your kindness, your acceptance, and your analysis. It's because of you that I ditch clichés and do my best to brainstorm. It's also because of you that I've always had a beanbag when times have gotten tough. Ms. Chambers, Mrs. Higgins, and Ms. Mysko, for letting me mold my words into laughter and beauty, and making sure that I had no fear. ~~Also, shout out to Ms. Mysko, as I am currently writing this in a workshop period in her class.~~ Ms. Haley and the members of UNITED, thank you for letting me laugh with you, and thank you for letting me cry. Helaine, for the tea, the coffee, and the encouragement.

Mom and Dad, for the wild and not-so-wild college stories that gave this book some foundation. Thank you for talking me up to co-workers, teaching me to walk so that I could learn to fly, and encouraging me to write in the first place. Meaghan, who I know can go on to do something great. Thank you for staying a kid in this boring world of adults.

Dr. Pepper soda and the light of my computer screen, for ensuring that I can write at 3 am.

And, of course, thank you dear reader, for making it this far. I only read the acknowledgement pages for writers that I enjoy, so thank you for tolerating my creation enough to read this. Also thank you for the ten dollars, unless you stole this book, in which I retract all my prior compliments directed toward you.

Author's Note:

Sometimes, you sit down and think to yourself, "I've never been to college, but screw it, I'm going to write about it anyway." Naturally, this happened to me in the winter of my junior year, because when you're reaching the end of high school, you're going to romanticize college. That's how life works. However, I didn't want to romanticize college, because I didn't want to be disappointed when I reach it and realize that it's not completely great. That is exactly why I wanted to hone in on how to establish that these characters aren't exactly sure what they should be doing.

They've moved to a new place by themselves, are staying on the school campus, and have little more to their names than clothing and whatever their parents were willing to give them in cash. I wanted to show how you can feel so incredibly small in such an unfamiliar situation, and I confess that perhaps this is a coping mechanism for the fact that this will be me next year.

Of course, I wasn't going to write about someone that everyone's seen before, like the football star, the frat boy, the typical sorority mean girl, or the classic nerd. Those people's stories have been told in bad 80's sitcoms and ABC family movies. What I wanted was to talk about the kids who fly under the radar, the ones who could very well have existed on your college campus, but you didn't know much beyond them other than that they drank too much or had weird hair or hardly ever left their dorms. I wanted to show that these people are just as valid as valedictorians and Heisman trophy winners. I like to think that to be an average, unremarkable person is to be an oxymoron and a fallacy, because every person has a thought and a world and a story to tell.

About the Author:

Kay Caswell is a person with eyes, a mouth, a nose, and hair that changes colors. She currently wanders around the Baltimore County area, specifically Reisterstown and Towson, but is bound for Some City, Somewhere within the next year. Besides writing poetry, she enjoys writing plays and creative nonfiction. In her free time, she draws, plays piano, and accumulates too many sweaters. She would like to become a Social Worker and a cosmetologist, both while continuing to pursue writing.

She has an angry resting face, eats too much pasta, and is able to juggle. She speaks a decent amount of a handful of languages, but has trouble with math unless she woke up on time, got at least 7 hours of sleep, and the moon is 77% full and directly overhead. She appreciates anyone who takes the time to listen, and hopes to one day possess that same grace in a constructive way.

Made in the USA
Middletown, DE
19 April 2016